SOLVE ET COAGULA

This is for you.
This book has made its way to you at a perfect time in your life.
It will challenge you in many ways.
Challenge you to grow.
Challenge you to feel.
Challenge you to reflect.
And hardest of all, challenge you to be completely honest with yourself.

100 days of shadow work isnt easy. One day isnt easy.
But every page completed is a step toward a more fulfilled & whole version of you.

So be proud of yourself & write as much as you can.
Congradulations on your willingness to go on this path of self discovery.

May this book serve as a torch that illuminates every crevice of your soul.

Shine a light on it all.

With love,
Muddy

What is Shadow Work?

Shadow work is the process of exploring subconscious behaviors, thoughts, patterns, and reactions to facilitate growth in an individual. We challenge ourselves in shadow work to be honest and transparent with ourselves. It's not easy to face ourselves in the mirror. It's not easy to look at aspects of ourselves that are toxic or embarrassing. But we know deep down that its worth doing for the sake of growth and self-improvement.

What we want is to be at peace. To look at our reflection and be able to say we are someone we are proud of.

In shadow work, we analyze ourselves and explore what behaviors and thoughts work in our favor or against us. If we discover something that doesn't serve our highest good, we actively choose to let it go and restructure ourself.

On the following pages are 100 days of questions to reflect on. Do one page every night. You dont have to do them in consecutive days, but challenge yourself to do them until you've completed the book. Write as much as you can on every page. Give yourself the opportunity to adjust behaviors that you dont like.

If you come across a prompt that is particularly hard to address, take your time. Feel what you feel. Do whatever you need to do, but its encouraged that you get through it to the best of your ability. It's understood that some of these questions may be uncomfortable, but no one said shadow work was easy.

On the corner of each page will be a list of different aspects of your life to keep in mind while you journal. Reference the list to make sure you're addressing as much as yourself as possible.

Do your best and you'll be your best.

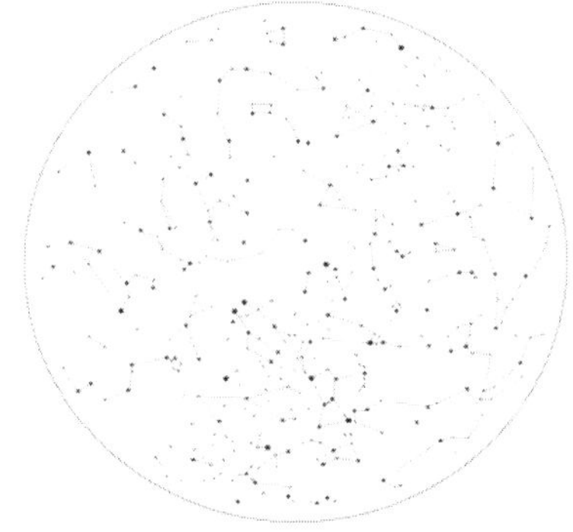

On this graph, rate each category on a scale from 1-10 (one being least satisfied and 10 being the most satisfied) of how content you are at present. You'll do this again at the end of the book when you've completed 100 days of shadow work. After you've scored yourself, write one sentence for each category discussing why you scored yourself the way you have on the next page. Here is an example. Below the example is a blank one for you.

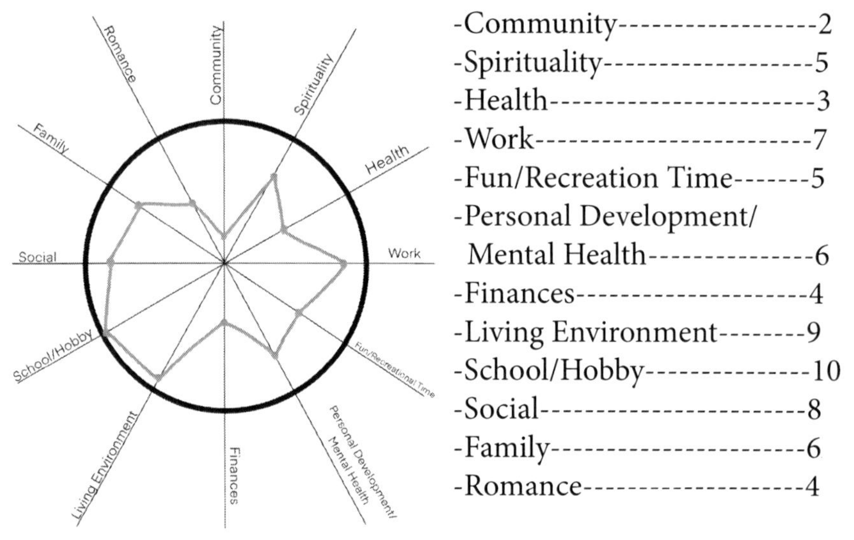

-Community-----------------2
-Spirituality-------------------5
-Health-----------------------3
-Work------------------------7
-Fun/Recreation Time-------5
-Personal Development/
Mental Health---------------6
-Finances--------------------4
-Living Environment--------9
-School/Hobby---------------10
-Social-----------------------8
-Family----------------------6
-Romance-------------------4

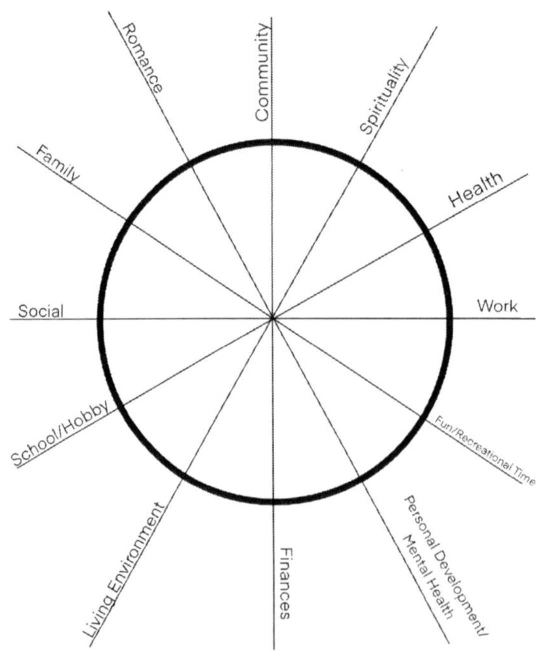

Community-

Spirituality-

Health-

Work-

Fun/Recreation Time-

Personal Development/Mental Health-

Finances-

Living Environment-

School/Hobby-

Social-

Family-

Romance-

WHAT BROUGHT YOU TO THE POINT OF WANTING TO DO SHADOW WORK? WHAT ARE YOU HOPING TO GET OUT OF THIS EXPERIENCE?

AM I OKAY WITH WHO I AM? LIST THE THINGS YOU'RE CONTENT WITH AND THE THINGS YOU'RE NOT. THINK ABOUT INTERACTIONS WITH OTHERS, CAREER GOALS, SELF TALK, ETC.

WHAT ARE SOME THINGS THAT MY FRIENDS/FAMILY HAVE GOTTEN MAD AT ME FOR? WAS IT REASONABLE? IS IT SOMETHING I CAN WORK ON?

WHAT CHARACTER TRAITS AM I THE MOST PROUD OF? HOW DO I DEMONSTRATE THOSE THINGS ON A DAILY BASIS?

WHAT CHARACTER TRAITS DO I RECOGNIZE AS TOXIC OR UNHEALTHY? WHY DO I DO THOSE THINGS? WHERE DO THOSE TRAITS COME FROM?

WHAT CAN I DO TO TURN INTO A PERSON I WOULD BE COMPLETELY PROUD OF?

WHAT TYPES OF CHARACTER TRAITS DO I ADMIRE IN OTHERS? WHY DO I ADMIRE THOSE THINGS SO MUCH?

WHAT ARE MY BIGGEST FEARS? ARE THEY RATIONAL? WHY DO I FEAR THOSE THINGS?

WHAT MAKES ME FEEL OUT OF CONTROL? REMEMBER TO CONSIDER THE THINGS MENTIONED ON THE LIST TO THE RIGHT OF EACH PAGE.

DO I DISLIKE FEELING OUT OF CONTROL? WHY DO I HOLD ONTO CONTROL? WHAT WOULD HAPPEN IF I LET GO OF THAT CONTROL FOR A MOMENT? HOW WOULD IT FEEL?

WHAT WOULD I CONSIDER TO BE ONE OF LIFE'S BIGGEST FAILURES? WHY?

HOW DO I FEEL WHEN I THINK I'VE FAILED SOMETHING? DO I TRY AGAIN? HOW DIFFICULT IS IT FOR ME TO REAPPROACH AND ATTEPMT A GOAL?
WHAT IS MY PATTERN WITH HOW I HANDLE FAILURE?

DO I ACCEPT THAT MY THOUGHTS DO NOT DEFINE ME AND THAT I CAN OBSERVE THEM AS JUST THOUGHTS? "I" AM THINKING. THEREFORE, "I" AM NOT MY THOUGHTS.

DO I ACCEPT THAT MY EMOTIONS DO NOT DEFINE ME AND THAT I CAN NOTE THEM WITHOUT ACTING ON THEM?

IS THERE ANYONE I HATE? WHY DO I HATE THEM? CAN I LET THAT EVENT GO AS A LEARNING LESSON?

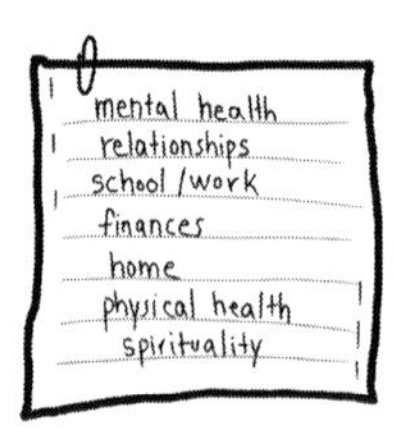

IN WHAT WAYS DO I HOLD MYSELF TO A HIGHER STANDARD THAN OTHERS?

DO I EVER GIVE ADVICE I CAN'T FOLLOW? WHY IS THAT SO?

AM I IMPORTANT TO MYSELF? CAN I PRIORITIZE MYSELF MORE?

ON A SCALE OF ONE TO TEN, HOW IMPORTANT IS BEING HAPPY? WHAT DOES IT TAKE TO BE HAPPY?

ON A SCALE OF ONE TO TEN, HOW HAPPY AM I? WHAT CAN I DO TO IMPROVE THIS SCORE EVEN HALF OF A POINT?

HOW CAN I MOVE FORWARD FROM A NEGATIVE SITUATION IN MY LIFE RIGHT NOW? IS THERE ANOTHER WAY THAT I CAN LOOK AT A NEGATIVE SITUATION GOING ON IN MY LIFE RIGHT NOW?

WHAT PERCENTAGE OF MY SELF TALK IS NEGATIVE VERSUS POSITIVE? IN WHAT SITUATIONS AM I COMFORTABLE WITH POSITIVE SELF TALK? IN WHAT SITUATIONS DO I TEND TO HAVE MORE NEGATIVE SELF TALK? HOW CAN I IMPROVE IN THE MOMENTS I FIND MYSELF PUTTING MYSELF DOWN?

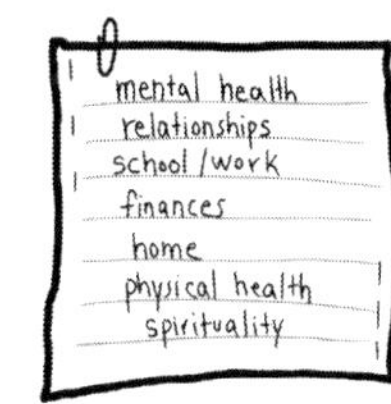

WHAT IS SOMETHING I AM GRATEFUL TO MY MOM FOR TEACHING ME?

WHAT IS SOMETHING I AM GRATEFUL TO MY DAD FOR TEACHING ME?

WHAT IS SOMETHING I WISH MY PARENTS WOULDN'T HAVE DONE? WHY?

WHAT LONG TERM EFFECTS HAS THAT EVENT HAD THAT THEY AREN'T AWARE OF?

WHAT IS SOMETHING YOU WISH YOU COULD EXPRESS TO YOUR PARENTS THAT YOU AREN'T QUITE SURE HOW TO VERBALIZE OUT LOUD?

WHAT IS SOMETHING YOU WISH YOU COULD EXPRESS TO A FRIEND OR PARTNER WHAT YOU AREN'T QUITE SURE HOW TO VERBALIZE OUT LOUD?

DO I GET EMBARRASSED EASILY? JOURNAL ABOUT A TIME THAT WAS EMBARASSING. WOULD YOU LAUGH AT ANOTHER PERSON IF IT HAPPENED TO THEM?

DO I SEEK APPROVAL FROM OTHERS? WHO? WHY DO I WANT OTHERS' APPROVAL SO BADLY?

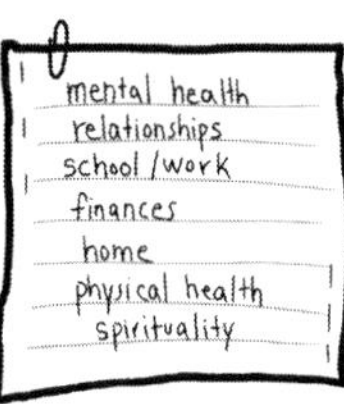

IS THERE ANYTHING I DO OR SAY THAT DOESN'T QUITE FEEL LIKE "ME?"

DO I AVOID MY EMOTIONS? TALK ABOUT A TIME IT FELT "EASIER" TO AVOID AN EMOTION THAN IT WAS TO SIT IN AN EMOTION.

DO I UNDERSTAND THE IMPORTANCE OF EMOTIONS? WHAT IS THE IMPORTANCE? HOW DO EMOTIONS BENEFIT ME?

AM I CONTENT WITH MY PHYSICAL BODY AND PHYSICAL SURROUNDINGS?

IN WHAT WAYS CAN I IMPROVE MY HEALTH AND MY PHYSICAL SURROUNDINGS?

AM I CONTENT WITH THE EMOTIONS I HAVE BEEN FEELING LATELY?

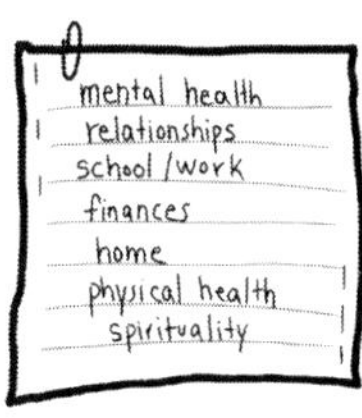

IN WHAT WAYS DO I LET MY EMOTIONS LEAD ME?

IN WHAT WAYS DO I PROJECT MY THOUGHTS AND EMOTIONS ONTO SITUATIONS AND MAKE IT WORSE THAN WHAT'S REALLY HAPPENING?

AM I IN CONTROL OF MY THOUGHTS TODAY? ARE MY THOUGHTS LOGICAL? DO I TEND TO CATASTROPHIZE EVENTS OR "FORTUNE TELL" THAT A SITUATION MAY TURN OUT BADLY?

AM I ABLE TO STAY FOCUSED FOR VERY LONG? IF NOT, WHAT IS DISTRACTING ME?

IN WHAT WAYS HAVE I FALLEN SHORT WITH MY GOALS THIS WEEK? CAN I FORGIVE MYSSELF FOR THIS OR DO I NEED TO MAKE UP FOR IT IN SOME OTHER WAY?

WHATS SOMETHING I CAN DO NEXT WEEK TO IMPROVE OR MEET MY GOALS?

HOW CAN I BE KINDER TO MYSELF TODAY? HOW OFTEN AM I TAKING MOMENTS TO TREAT MYSELF?

IF NOTHING ELSE GETS DONE TODAY, WHAT'S THE ONE THING I CAN ACCOMPLISH AND FEEL FULFILLED BY DOING?

IN WHAT WAYS DO I PUNISH MYSELF? EMOTIONALLY? MENTALLY? PHYSICALLY?

IF I WERE TO MEET MYSELF, WOULD I WANT TO BE MY OWN FRIEND?

CAN I SAY THAT I TRY MY HARDEST?

HAS ANYONE EVER SAID THAT I AM ARROGANT? WHY DID THEY SAY THAT?

HOW DO I HANDLE CRITICISM?

DO I HAVE A TENDENCY TO POINT THE FINGER BACK AT SOMEONE WHO IS UPSET WITH ME?

DO I TAKE ACCOUNTABILITY WHEN I HAVE MESSED UP?

AM I ABLE TO APOLOGIZE WHEN I HAVE HURT SOMEONE? WHAT DO MY APOLOGIES SOUND LIKE? DO I NEED TO ELABORATE ON THEM MORE?

DO I USE HUMOR TO COVER UP INSECURITIES? WHAT ARE MY INSECURITIES?

DO I TAKE ON TOO MANY PROJECTS AT THE SAME TIME? DO I ATTACH MY VALUE TO THE AMOUNT OF WORK I DO OR ACCOMPLISHMENTS I HAVE?

WHEN SOMEONE DOESN'T AGREE WITH ME, DO I ARGUE BACK WITH FACTS OR INSULTS?

WHY DO I FEEL THE NEED TO CONVINCE OTHERS TO SEE THINGS THE SAME WAY I DO?

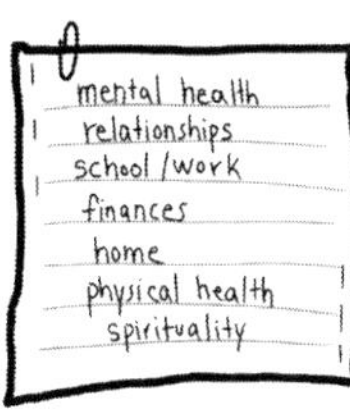

WHAT BOTHERS ME THE MOST ABOUT OTHER PEOPLE?

DESCRIBE YOUR PERFECT BEST FRIEND. DO I HAVE THAT PERSON IN MY LIFE?

DESCRIBE YOUR PERFECT ROMANTIC PARTNER. DO I HAVE THAT PERSON IN MY LIFE?

ARE THOSE TRAITS YOU POSSESS YOURSELF?

mental health
relationships
school/work
finances
home
physical health
spirituality

WHAT DO YOU THINK YOU NEED TO WORK ON THE MOST?

DISSECT AN UNHEALTHY HABIT YOU HAVE. WHEN DID IT START? WHY? HOW DOES IT AFFECT YOUR LIFE?

WHAT TYPE OF CAREER DO YOU THINK WORKS BEST FOR YOUR PERSONALITY TYPE?

WHAT ARE SOME CORE VALUES YOU HAVE? WHERE DID THEY COME FROM?

HOW DO YOU FEEL WHEN OTHERS DON'T HAVE THE SAME VALUES?

DO YOU CONSIDER YOURSELF A GOOD PERSON? IS BEING A GOOD PERSON IMPORTANT TO YOU? HOW DO YOU WANT TO BE REMEMBERED?

IN WHAT WAYS HAVE YOU SACRIFICED FOR OTHERS?

IN WHAT WAYS DO YOU SUFFER?

DO YOU THINK THAT SUFFERING IS NECESSARY FOR GROWTH?

WHEN YOU ARE NOT DOING WELL EMOTIONALLY, DO YOU KEEP IN MIND THAT IT'S TEMPORARY?

WHAT IS AN AFFIRMATION OR PHRASE THAT HELPS YOU THROUGH TOUGH TIMES? WHY DOES IT RESONATE WITH YOU?

DO YOU FEEL LIKE ANYTHING IS LACKING IN YOUR LIFE?

HOW CAN I ATTRACT OTHERS INTO MY LIFE?

WHAT IS SOMETHING THAT I AM CONSTANTLY RUNNING AWAY FROM?

ARE THERE ANY MEMORIES YOU HAVE THAT ARE DIFFICULT TO THINK ABOUT?

WITHOUT DISSECTING THE EVENTS OF THAT MEMORY, HOW DID THAT MEMORY MAKE YOU FEEL?

IS THERE ANYTHING I NEED TO FORGIVE MYSELF FOR?

IN WHAT WAYS HAVE I GROWN FROM LAST YEAR?

THINK ABOUT A BAD RELATIONSHIP YOU'VE HAD. WHAT LESSONS CAN YOU TAKE AWAY FROM IT?

DO I TREAT OTHERS THE WAY I WANT TO BE TREATED?

DO I TREAT MY PARTNER THE SAME WAY I WOULD TREAT MY FRIENDS WHEN IM ANGRY?

IF I COULD GIVE ADVICE TO MY YOUNGER SELF, WHAT WOULD IT BE?

WHAT IS SOMETHING YOU DON'T WANT TO REGRET ON YOUR DEATH BED?

IN WHAT SMALL WAY CAN I MOVE TOWARD ONE OF MY GOALS TODAY?

DO I FEEL MORE MASCULINE OR FEMININE?

IN WHAT WAYS CAN I BRING MY MASCULINE AND FEMININE SIDE CLOSER TO A BALANCED CENTER?

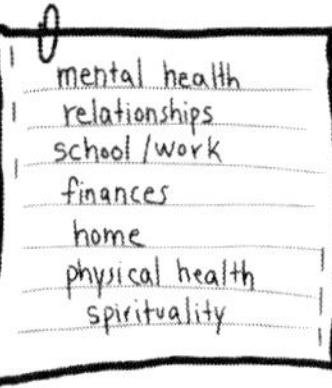

IS THERE ANYTHING THAT'S BEEN SAID TO ME LATELY THAT I MAY HAVE MISINTERPRETED?

HOW CAN I MAKE THE SPACE AROUND ME A LITTLE NICER TODAY?

AM I HEAVILY AFFECTED BY THE SEASONS?

HAVE I SPENT ANY TIME OUTDOORS LATELY? DO I FIND COMFORT IN BEING IN NATURE OR INSIDE? WHAT DOES BEING OUTSIDE DO FOR US AS HUMANS?

DO I HAVE ANY VICES I CAN LIVE WITHOUT?

IS THERE ANY PART OF ME THAT IS HARD TO ACCEPT ABOUT MYSELF?

HAS THERE EVER BEEN A RELATIONSHIP IN MY LIFE THAT DIDN'T TURN OUT THE WAY I WANTED IT TO?

IN WHAT WAYS DID I PLAY A ROLE IN THE DOWNFALL OF THAT RELATIONSHIP?

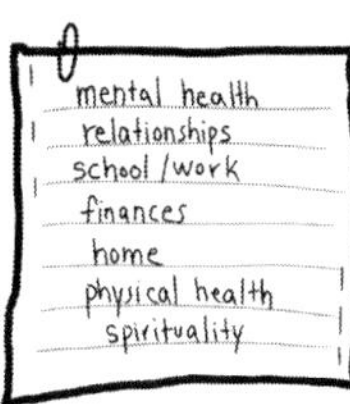

AM I PROUD OF THE WAY I'VE RESPONDED TO CONFLICT IN MY RELATIONSHIPS?

DO I HAVE ANY TOXIC QUALITIES I CAN IMPROVE ON?

WHAT IS SOMETHING THAT I COULD NEVER FORGIVE SOMEONE FOR?

HOW IMPORTANT IS HONESTY?

DO I GOSSIP ABOUT PEOPLE? WHAT DOES IT ADD TO MY LIFE IF I DO?

IF I COULD GET RID OF ONE MEMORY, WHAT WOULD IT BE AND WHY?

Congratulations on completing 100 days of shadow work. Some of the questions may have been difficult to answer. Some you may have had to go back and add onto. Use this page and the next to reflect on what changes you've noticed in yourself since starting this journey. Complete this graph now that you've reached the end and compare it to the first one you did at the beginning of this book.

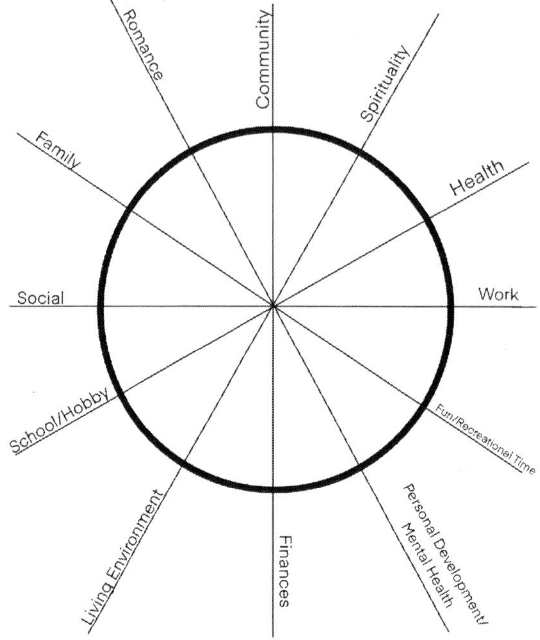

Community-

Spirituality-

Health-

Work-

Fun/Recreation Time-

Personal Development/Mental Health-

Finances-

Living Environment-

School/Hobby-

Social-

Family-

Romance-